IT'S ALWAYS WINE O'CLOCK

Andrews McMeel
Publishing®

a division of Andrews McMeel Universal

TO..

FROM..

NOW IS THE TIME FOR DRINKING!

Horace

WINE IS THE MOST CIVILIZED THING IN THE WORLD.

Ernest Hemingway

ALCOHOL MAY BE
MAN'S WORST ENEMY,
BUT THE BIBLE SAYS
LOVE YOUR ENEMY.

Frank Sinatra

THERE ARE TWO THINGS
A HIGHLANDER LIKES
NAKED, AND ONE OF
THEM IS MALT WHISKY.

Scottish proverb

SOBRIETY DIMINISHES,
DISCRIMINATES, AND
SAYS NO; DRUNKENNESS
EXPANDS, UNITES,
AND SAYS YES.

William James

CLARET IS THE
LIQUOR FOR BOYS;
PORT, FOR MEN; BUT HE
WHO ASPIRES TO BE A
HERO ... MUST DRINK
BRANDY.

Samuel Johnson

AH, DRINK AGAIN
THIS RIVER THAT IS THE
TAKER-AWAY OF PAIN,
AND THE GIVER-BACK
OF BEAUTY!

Edna St. Vincent Millay

HERE'S TO THE
CORKSCREW—A USEFUL
KEY TO UNLOCK THE
STOREHOUSE OF WIT,
THE TREASURY OF
LAUGHTER, THE FRONT
DOOR OF FELLOWSHIP,
AND THE GATE OF
PLEASANT FOLLY.

W. E. P. French

IT'S 4:58
ON FRIDAY
AFTERNOON.
DO YOU KNOW
WHERE YOUR
MARGARITA IS?

Amy Neftzger

NO ANIMAL EVER INVENTED ANYTHING SO BAD AS DRUNKENNESS— OR SO GOOD AS DRINK.

G. K. Chesterton

A WALTZ AND A
GLASS OF WINE INVITE
AN ENCORE.

Johann Strauss

ALL IS FAIR IN LOVE AND BEER.

Anonymous

ALCOHOL IS NOT THE
ANSWER TO LIFE'S
QUESTION. . . . IT HELPS
YOU FORGET THE
QUESTION.

Vijay Mallya

WHENEVER A MAN
IS TIRED, WINE IS A
GREAT RESTORER OF
STRENGTH.

Homer

I ONLY TAKE A DRINK ON TWO OCCASIONS: WHEN I'M THIRSTY AND WHEN I'M NOT.

Brendan Behan

WINE IMPROVES WITH
AGE. THE OLDER I GET,
THE BETTER I LIKE IT.

Anonymous

THE SOFT EXTRACTIVE
NOTE OF AN AGED CORK
BEING WITHDRAWN HAS
THE TRUE SOUND OF A
MAN OPENING HIS HEART.

William S. Benwell

COME, LANDLORD,
FILL A FLOWING BOWL
UNTIL IT DOES RUN OVER,
TONIGHT WE WILL
ALL MERRY BE—
TOMORROW WE'LL
GET SOBER.

John Fletcher

TOO MUCH CHABLIS CAN MAKE YOU WHABLIS.

Ogden Nash

ONE NOT ONLY DRINKS
THE WINE, ONE SMELLS
IT, OBSERVES IT, TASTES
IT, SIPS IT, AND ONE
TALKS ABOUT IT.

King Edward VII

FERMENTATION EQUALS CIVILIZATION.

John Ciardi

TEETOTALLERS LACK
THE SYMPATHY AND
GENEROSITY OF MEN
THAT DRINK.

W. H. Davies

THE DRINK YOU LIKE THE BEST SHOULD BE THE DRINK YOU DRINK THE MOST.

J. B. Burgess

CHAMPAGNE IS ONE OF THE ELEGANT EXTRAS IN LIFE.

Charles Dickens

A HANGOVER IS THE
WRATH OF GRAPES.

Anonymous

A MAN OUGHT TO GET
DRUNK AT LEAST TWICE
A YEAR . . . SO HE WON'T
LET HIMSELF GET
SNOTTY ABOUT IT.

Raymond Chandler

WHEN I DRINK,
I THINK; AND
WHEN I THINK,
I DRINK.

François Rabelais

ONLY IRISH COFFEE
PROVIDES IN A SINGLE
GLASS ALL FOUR
ESSENTIAL FOOD GROUPS:
ALCOHOL, CAFFEINE,
SUGAR, AND FAT.

Anonymous

WHETHER WINE
IS NOURISHMENT,
MEDICINE, OR POISON IS
A MATTER OF DOSAGE.

Paracelsus

THE ONLY AMERICAN INVENTION AS PERFECT AS THE SONNET.

H. L. Mencken on the martini

QUAINTEST THOUGHTS—
QUEEREST FANCIES COME TO
LIFE AND FADE AWAY;
WHAT CARE I HOW
TIME ADVANCES?
I AM DRINKING ALE TODAY.

Edgar Allan Poe

ALCOHOL MAY NOT
SOLVE YOUR PROBLEMS,
BUT NEITHER WILL
WATER OR MILK.

Anonymous

KEEPING ONE'S GUESTS
SUPPLIED WITH LIQUOR
IS THE FIRST LAW OF
HOSPITALITY.

Margaret Way

GOOD WINE IS A
GOOD FAMILIAR
CREATURE IF IT
BE WELL USED.

William Shakespeare

THE CHURCH IS NEAR,
BUT THE ROAD IS ICY.
THE BAR IS FAR, BUT I
WILL WALK CAREFULLY.

Russian proverb

FROM WINE WHAT SUDDEN FRIENDSHIP SPRINGS.

John Gay

I SPENT NINETY
PERCENT OF MY MONEY
ON WINE, WOMEN,
AND SONG AND JUST
WASTED THE OTHER
TEN PERCENT.

Ronnie Hawkins

GOD MADE YEAST, AS
WELL AS DOUGH, AND
LOVES FERMENTATION
JUST AS DEARLY AS HE
LOVES VEGETATION.

Ralph Waldo Emerson

ON SOME DAYS, MY HEAD
IS FILLED WITH SUCH
WILD AND ORIGINAL
THOUGHTS THAT I CAN
BARELY UTTER A WORD.
ON OTHER DAYS, THE
LIQUOR STORE IS CLOSED.

Frank Varano

THE SHARPER IS THE BERRY, THE SWEETER IS THE WINE.

Proverb

IF ON MY THEME I
RIGHTLY THINK,
THERE ARE FIVE REASONS
WHY MEN DRINK,—
GOOD WINE, A FRIEND,
BECAUSE I'M DRY,
OR LEST I SHOULD
BE BY AND BY,
OR ANY OTHER REASON WHY.

Jean Sirmond

IN WINE THERE IS
WISDOM, IN BEER THERE
IS FREEDOM, IN WATER
THERE IS BACTERIA.

Unknown

I LIKE TO DRINK
MARTINIS. TWO, AT THE
MOST. THREE, I'M UNDER
THE TABLE; FOUR, I'M
UNDER THE HOST.

Dorothy Parker

IF THIS DOG DO
YOU BITE, SOON AS OUT
OF YOUR BED, TAKE A
HAIR OF THE TAIL IN
THE MORNING.

Scottish proverb

WINE TO ME IS
PASSION. . . . WINE IS
ART. IT'S CULTURE.
IT'S THE ESSENCE OF
CIVILIZATION AND THE
ART OF LIVING.

Robert Mondavi

JUST THE
SIMPLE ACT OF
TASTING A GLASS
OF WINE IS ITS
OWN EVENT.

David Hyde Pierce

ALCOHOL, TAKEN IN
SUFFICIENT QUANTITIES,
MAY PRODUCE ALL
THE EFFECTS OF
DRUNKENNESS.

Oscar Wilde

BURGUNDY MAKES YOU
THINK OF SILLY THINGS,
BORDEAUX MAKES YOU
TALK OF THEM, AND
CHAMPAGNE MAKES
YOU DO THEM.

Jean Anthelme Brillat-Savarin

I LOVE TO SING. AND
I LOVE TO DRINK SCOTCH.
MOST PEOPLE WOULD
RATHER HEAR ME
DRINK SCOTCH.

George Burns

MEET ME DOWN IN
THE BAR! WE'LL DRINK
BREAKFAST TOGETHER.

W. C. Fields

RED WINE IS JUST LIKE KETCHUP: IT GOES WITH EVERYTHING.

Jason Walton

DRINK WINE, AND YOU
WILL SLEEP WELL.
SLEEP, AND YOU WILL
NOT SIN. AVOID SIN, AND
YOU WILL BE SAVED.
ERGO, DRINK WINE
AND BE SAVED.

Medieval German proverb

THERE'S NAUGHT, NO
DOUBT, SO MUCH THE
SPIRIT CALMS AS RUM
AND TRUE RELIGION:
THUS IT WAS.

Lord Byron

THE SECRET TO
ENJOYING A GOOD WINE:
OPEN THE BOTTLE TO
ALLOW IT TO BREATHE. IF
IT DOES NOT LOOK LIKE
IT'S BREATHING, GIVE IT
MOUTH-TO-MOUTH.

Anonymous

WINE IS THE THINKING PERSON'S HEALTH DRINK.

Philip Norrie

THE PROBLEM WITH A TREADMILL IS THAT THE ICE FALLS OUT OF YOUR GLASS.

Bruce Tomlinson

I DRINK WHEN I
HAVE OCCASION, AND
SOMETIMES WHEN I
HAVE NO OCCASION.

Miguel de Cervantes

COMPROMISES ARE FOR RELATIONSHIPS, NOT WINE.

Robert Scott Caywood

IF FOOD IS THE BODY
OF GOOD LIVING,
WINE IS ITS SOUL.

Clifton Fadiman

LET SCHOOLMASTERS
PUZZLE THEIR BRAIN
WITH GRAMMAR, AND
NONSENSE, AND LEARNING,
GOOD LIQUOR,
I STOUTLY MAINTAIN,
GIVES GENIUS A BETTER
DISCERNING.

Oliver Goldsmith

WHEN A MAN DRINKS
WINE AT DINNER, HE
BEGINS TO BE BETTER
PLEASED WITH HIMSELF.

Plato

REALITY IS AN ILLUSION CREATED BY A LACK OF ALCOHOL.

Anonymous

FINE WINE IS A LIVING LIQUID CONTAINING NO PRESERVATIVES.

Julia Child

NEVER TRUST A MAN
WHO DOESN'T DRINK.

James Crumley

FAN THE SINKING
FLAME OF HILARITY
WITH THE WING OF
FRIENDSHIP; AND PASS
THE ROSY WINE.

Charles Dickens

MY ONLY REGRET IS
THAT I HAVE NOT DRUNK
MORE CHAMPAGNE
IN MY LIFE.

John Maynard Keynes

WINE MAKES DAILY
LIVING EASIER, LESS
HURRIED, WITH FEWER
TENSIONS AND MORE
TOLERANCE.

Benjamin Franklin

I HAVE LIVED
TEMPERATELY. . . .
I DOUBLE THE DOCTOR'S
RECOMMENDATION OF
A GLASS AND A HALF
OF WINE EACH DAY AND
EVEN TREBLE IT WITH
A FRIEND.

Thomas Jefferson

THE WORSE YOU ARE AT THINKING, THE BETTER YOU ARE AT DRINKING.

Terry Goodkind

WINE REJOICES THE
HEART OF MAN AND JOY
IS THE MOTHER OF
ALL VIRTUES.

Johann Wolfgang von Goethe

THERE'S ALCOHOL
IN PLANT AND TREE.
IT MUST BE
NATURE'S PLAN
THAT THERE SHOULD BE
IN FAIR DEGREE
SOME ALCOHOL IN MAN.

A. P. Herbert

I NEVER TASTE
THE WINE FIRST IN
RESTAURANTS, I JUST
ASK THE WAITER
TO POUR.

Nigella Lawson

WHAT I LIKE TO DRINK MOST IS WINE THAT BELONGS TO OTHERS.

Diogenes the Cynic

BUT I'M NOT SO THINK
AS YOU DRUNK I AM.

J. C. Squire

ALE, MAN, ALE'S THE STUFF TO DRINK FOR FELLOWS WHOM IT HURTS TO THINK.

A. E. Housman

I DON'T GET DRUNK,
I GET AWESOME.

Anonymous

SOBER OR BLOTTO, THIS IS YOUR MOTTO: KEEP MUDDLING THROUGH.

P. G. Wodehouse

THERE ST. JOHN MINGLES
WITH MY FRIENDLY BOWL
THE FEAST OF REASON
AND THE FLOW OF SOUL.

Alexander Pope

A GOURMET MEAL
WITHOUT A GLASS OF
WINE JUST SEEMS
TRAGIC TO ME SOMEHOW.

Kathy Mattea

THERE IS NO SUCH
THING AS BAD WHISKY.
SOME WHISKIES JUST
HAPPEN TO BE BETTER
THAN OTHERS.

William Faulkner

I HAVE TAKEN MORE OUT OF ALCOHOL THAN ALCOHOL HAS TAKEN OUT OF ME.

Winston Churchill

THE PROBLEM WITH
THE WORLD IS THAT
EVERYONE IS A FEW
DRINKS BEHIND.

Humphrey Bogart

POUR OUT THE WINE
WITHOUT RESTRAINT
OR STAY;
POUR NOT BY CUPS, BUT
BY THE BELLYFUL;
POUR OUT TO ALL
THAT WULL.

Edmund Spenser

IT TAKES ONLY ONE
DRINK TO GET ME
DRUNK. THE TROUBLE
IS, I CAN'T REMEMBER
IF IT'S THE THIRTEENTH
OR THE FOURTEENTH.

George Burns

WINE . . . THE INTELLECTUAL PART OF THE MEAL.

Alexandre Dumas

WINE, TAKEN IN
MODERATION, MAKES
LIFE, FOR A MOMENT,
BETTER, AND WHEN THE
MOMENT PASSES LIFE
DOES NOT FOR THAT
REASON BECOME WORSE.

Bernard Levin

YOUR BODY IS A TEMPLE.
YOU SHOULD KEEP SOME
SPIRITS IN YOU.

Bruce Tomlinson

BEAUTY IS IN THE EYE
OF THE BEER HOLDER.

Anonymous

WHY DON'T YOU GET
OUT OF THOSE WET
CLOTHES AND INTO A
DRY MARTINI.

Robert Benchley

QUICKLY, BRING ME
A BEAKER OF WINE,
SO THAT I MAY WET
MY MIND AND SAY
SOMETHING CLEVER.

Aristophanes

I BELIEVE THAT IF
LIFE GIVES YOU LEMONS,
YOU SHOULD MAKE
LEMONADE. AND TRY TO
FIND SOMEBODY WHOSE
LIFE HAS GIVEN THEM
VODKA, AND HAVE.
A PARTY.

Ron White

GOOD COMPANY, GOOD WINE, GOOD WELCOME, CAN MAKE GOOD PEOPLE.

William Shakespeare

ABSTAINER: A WEAK
PERSON WHO YIELDS TO
THE TEMPTATION OF
DENYING HIMSELF
A PLEASURE.

Ambrose Bierce

DRINK WHAT YOU WANT;
DRINK WHAT YOU'RE ABLE.
IF YOU ARE DRINKING
WITH ME,
YOU'LL BE UNDER
THE TABLE.

Anonymous

SORROW CAN BE
ALLEVIATED BY GOOD
SLEEP, A BATH, AND A
GLASS OF WINE.

Thomas Aquinas

THE PROPER UNION OF
GIN AND VERMOUTH IS
A GREAT AND SUDDEN
GLORY.

Bernard DeVoto

SOME FOLKS OF CIDER
MAKE A ROUT,
AND CIDER'S WELL
ENOUGH NO DOUBT,
WHEN BETTER LIQUORS FAIL;
BUT WINE, THAT'S RICHER,
BETTER STILL, EV'N
WINE ITSELF
(DENY'T WHO WILL)
MUST YIELD TO NAPPY ALE.

John Gay

EAT THY BREAD
WITH JOY, AND
DRINK THY WINE
WITH A MERRY
HEART.

Ecclesiastes 9:7

MAY YOUR GLASS
BE EVER FULL,
MAY THE ROOF OVER YOUR
HEAD BE ALWAYS STRONG,
AND MAY YOU BE IN HEAVEN
HALF AN HOUR BEFORE
THE DEVIL KNOWS
YOU'RE DEAD.

Irish toast

WHENEVER SOMEONE
ASKS ME IF I WANT
WATER WITH MY SCOTCH,
I SAY, "I'M THIRSTY,
NOT DIRTY."

Joe E. Lewis

WINE IS THE MOST HEALTHFUL AND MOST HYGIENIC OF BEVERAGES.

Louis Pasteur

WHAT HARM IN DRINKING
CAN THERE BE,
SINCE PUNCH AND LIFE
SO WELL AGREE?

Thomas Blacklock

WHERE THERE'S HOOCH, THERE'S HOPE.

Frank Kelly Rich

HAPPINESS IS A
DRY MARTINI AND A
GOOD WOMAN . . . OR
A BAD WOMAN.

George Burns

DRINKING IS A WAY OF ENDING THE DAY.

Ernest Hemingway

TO HAPPY CONVENTS,
BOSOMED DEEP IN VINES,
WHERE SLUMBER ABBOTS,
PURPLE AS THEIR WINES.

Alexander Pope

THERE IS A
COMMUNION OF MORE
THAN OUR BODIES WHEN
BREAD IS BROKEN AND
WINE DRUNK.

M. F. K. Fisher

IF A LIFE OF WINE,
WOMEN, AND SONG
BECOMES TOO MUCH,
GIVE UP THE SINGING.

Anonymous

WITHIN THE BOTTLE'S DEPTHS, THE WINE'S SOUL SANG ONE NIGHT.

Charles Baudelaire

MAN, BEING
REASONABLE, MUST
GET DRUNK;
THE BEST OF LIFE IS
BUT INTOXICATION.

Lord Byron

MAY OUR LOVE
BE LIKE GOOD WINE;
GROW STRONGER AS IT
GROWS OLDER.

Old English toast

THERE IS NOT THE
HUNDREDTH PART OF
THE WINE CONSUMED
IN THIS KINGDOM THAT
THERE OUGHT TO BE.
OUR FOGGY CLIMATE
WANTS HELP.

Jane Austen

THE BOURBON KING
WAS FIRST AMBASSADOR
OF REASON AND HUMAN
HAPPINESS.

Heinrich Mann

HABIT [HAS] RENDERED
THE LIGHT AND HIGH
FLAVORED WINES A
NECESSARY OF LIFE
WITH ME.

Thomas Jefferson

THE WINE CUP IS THE
LITTLE SILVER WELL
WHERE TRUTH, IF
TRUTH THERE BE, DOTH
EVER DWELL.

Edward FitzGerald

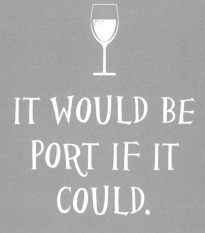

IT WOULD BE PORT IF IT COULD.

Richard Bentley on claret

A BUMPER OF GOOD
LIQUOR
WILL END A CONTEST
QUICKER
THAN JUSTICE, JUDGE,
OR VICAR.

Richard Brinsley Sheridan

LOVE MAKES THE WORLD
GO ROUND? NOT AT ALL.
WHISKY MAKES IT GO
ROUND TWICE AS FAST.

Compton Mackenzie

YOU HAVE TO DRINK,
OTHERWISE YOU'D GO
STARK STARING SOBER.

Keith Waterhouse

I DON'T HAVE A BEER
BELLY. IT'S A BURGUNDY
BELLY AND IT COST ME
A LOT OF MONEY.

Charles Clarke

CHAMPAGNE CERTAINLY
GIVES ONE WERRY
GENTLEMANLY
IDEAS, BUT FOR A
CONTINUANCE, I DON'T
KNOW BUT I SHOULD
PREFER MILD HALE.

R. S. Surtees

I'M ABC NOW.
ANYTHING BUT
CHARDONNAY.

John Major

WOMAN FIRST TEMPTED
MAN TO EAT; HE TOOK
TO DRINKING OF HIS
OWN ACCORD.

John R. Kemble

IF I HAD TO LIVE MY
LIFE OVER, I'D LIVE
OVER A SALOON.

W. C. Fields

GO, FETCH TO ME
A PINT O' WINE,
AND FILL IT IN A
SILVER TASSIE.

Robert Burns

LICKER TALKS MIGHTY
LOUD W'EN IT GIT LOOSE
FUM DE JUG.

Joel Chandler Harris

TOPPING BEER OFF WITH WINE—THAT'S FINE!

German proverb

THERE COMES A TIME IN
EVERY WOMAN'S LIFE
WHEN THE ONLY THING
THAT HELPS IS A GLASS
OF CHAMPAGNE.

Bette Davis

WINE IS SUNLIGHT, HELD TOGETHER BY WATER.

Galileo Galilei

I FEEL SORRY FOR
PEOPLE WHO DON'T
DRINK. WHEN THEY
WAKE UP IN THE
MORNING, THAT'S AS
GOOD AS THEY'RE GOING
TO FEEL ALL DAY.

Frank Sinatra

WHAT'S DRINKING?
A MERE PAUSE FROM
THINKING!

Lord Byron

BEER IS MADE BY MEN, WINE BY GOD!

Martin Luther

FILL EV'RY GLASS, FOR
WINE INSPIRES US,
AND FIRES US
WITH COURAGE, LOVE,
AND JOY.

John Gay

Here's to Alcohol, the Rose-Colored Glasses of Life.

F. Scott Fitzgerald

If you're interested in learning more
about our books, find us on Facebook at
Andrews McMeel Publishing and follow us
on Twitter: **@AndrewsMcMeel.**

www.andrewsmcmeel.com

Andrews McMeel Publishing
a division of Andrews McMeel Universal
1130 Walnut Street, Kansas City, Missouri 64106

www.andrewsmcmeel.com

15 16 17 18 19 SHO 10 9 8 7 6 5 4 3 2

ISBN: 978-1-4494-7120-0

Library of Congress Control Number: 2015935776

Published by arrangement with Summersdale Publishers Ltd.

ATTENTION: SCHOOLS AND BUSINESSES

Andrews McMeel books are available at quantity discounts
with bulk purchase for educational, business, or sales
promotional use. For information, please e-mail the
Andrews McMeel Publishing Special Sales Department:
specialsales@amuniversal.com.